BEI GRIN MACHT SICH IHR WISSEN BEZAHLT

AF151555

- Wir veröffentlichen Ihre Hausarbeit,
  Bachelor- und Masterarbeit

- Ihr eigenes eBook und Buch -
  weltweit in allen wichtigen Shops

- Verdienen Sie an jedem Verkauf

Jetzt bei www.GRIN.com hochladen und kostenlos publizieren

Richards Macdonald

Use of Information Technology in Local Governments

GRIN Verlag

Bibliografische Information der Deutschen Nationalbibliothek:

Die Deutsche Bibliothek verzeichnet diese Publikation in der Deutschen National-
bibliografie; detaillierte bibliografische Daten sind im Internet über http://dnb.d-
nb.de/ abrufbar.

Impressum:

Copyright © 2010 GRIN Verlag GmbH
Druck und Bindung: Books on Demand GmbH, Norderstedt Germany
ISBN: 978-3-656-43320-0

Dieses Buch bei GRIN:

http://www.grin.com/de/e-book/214973/use-of-information-technology-in-local-
governments

GRIN - Your knowledge has value

Der GRIN Verlag publiziert seit 1998 wissenschaftliche Arbeiten von Studenten, Hochschullehrern und anderen Akademikern als eBook und gedrucktes Buch. Die Verlagswebsite www.grin.com ist die ideale Plattform zur Veröffentlichung von Hausarbeiten, Abschlussarbeiten, wissenschaftlichen Aufsätzen, Dissertationen und Fachbüchern.

Besuchen Sie uns im Internet:

http://www.grin.com/

http://www.facebook.com/grincom

http://www.twitter.com/grin_com

Use of Information Technology in Local Governments

Nowadays, local and state government use of information technology has been manifested in several independent systems, each one satisfying one specific program need or supporting one business function. As a result of this, a large and rapidly growing number of individual systems are employed for government-to-government (G2G) business across local and state levels. Furthermore, this multiplicity of systems of often said to be a significant impediment to effective work. Additionally, it is also a strain from the financial perspective since many systems need their own software, hardware, office space, security, as well as business rules (Stenberg & Austin 2007) (Kim & Bretschneider 2006).

Therefore, in order to enable smooth performance of business functions on every system, local government personnel and officials are required to sign in and sign out when they use each system, demanding several log ins and passwords. Typically, data which is entered into one system cannot be used by other systems. Enormous number of duplicate requests for information are made and granted as independent individual organizations reply to uncoordinated requirements and requests, thereby posing a significant burden on the functioning and work processes of both local governments and state agencies and implies higher than required costs of every individual (Augustsan 2001).

As a solution to this bottleneck, the New York State-Local Internet Gateway Prototype was developed for testing an alternative strategy to this present way of working. The main objective of this Prototype was to determine, demonstrate, and measure the key factors that are associated with a single point of contact to enable G2G work amongst local and state governments.

Following in that direction, a largely representative group of local and state officials produced a vision for a perfect and ideal State-Local Gateway. These officials believed that an ideal State-Local gateway is:

1. driven by practical business needs
2. jointly governed by local and state organizations with the aid of a formal governing structure
3. designed to initiate ongoing costs and initial investments via future cost reductions to every participant
4. affordable to every interested participant
5. characterized by accurate, authentic, and high quality data
6. secured from internal misuse and external threats by jointly developed security features

7. constantly assessed for improvement and usability under various kinds of local conditions and employ a standard set of conventions for applications and information

8. designed from the end user's perspective

9. designed to adapt users having lower technical skills

10. capable of incorporating other existing efforts

11. easily available to every local and state user, and highly reliable (Kim & Bretschneider 2006).

The features were eventually adopted as core principles for guiding a prototyping effort in order to test the feasibility of a common contact for G2G work between local and state governments (Stenberg & Austin 2007).

Toward that end, the local governments have been using information technology for a long time; however, the level of capacity of information technology differs tremendously across local governments. While development of web-based E-government applications becomes increasingly prevalent, enforcing newly developed IT continues to rely on the usual ability of government to receive, manage as well as utilize IT (King 1982).

Improvising and enhancing the infrastructure for communications and information within local governments has remained a hard shell. Numerous ambitious public-sector projects in Information technology fail mainly due to the inadequacy of resources, impractical expectations, and the shortage of strong support from the upper force. Significantly, these are the findings of Research and Consulting Center of GFO in its regular work on local and state public agencies nationwide. However, the risk still persists to do nothing within the Information Age. Nowadays, consumers are rather accustomed to getting everything from the daily groceries to an MBA degree online. Instead of expressing dissatisfaction, the knowledgeable consumer might be exiting for better alternatives (Augustsan 2001).

Information technology employed by local government aims at addressing an entire range of concerns regarding public resource planners reflecting IT, not only implementation and procurement strategy but also practical applications of public-sector information systems. Practitioners have mined the current wealth arising from research in order to answer three basic questions:

1.   How and why a public agency is required to undertake the deployment and utilization of a modernized integrated information system?

2.   What are the other uses of technology apart from the storage of records, and where can we find examples of communities that use new technology to its maximum potential.

3.   What are the skills and tools required for a successful step towards information technology?

While the public-sector IT director may strive for making it all work, yet the task remains to find a way of selling the system to his or her seniors and to the general public. A consumer may, after all, not be inclined towards supporting new equipments and systems only to reduce wasted effort, time, and money. Nevertheless, that same consumer may get a better experience if those same systems could enable convenient payment of fines and taxes, check availability of a book in a library, provide access to real estate and property appraisals, eliminate faults and fraud at the ballot box, facilitate and speed up citizen complaints, and offer an aid for optimal execution of fire/ police services. Therefore, these demonstrate a few of the accomplishments of a vast number of communities for their progressive usage of information systems. Moreover, its been repeatedly stated that e-government is something more than a municipal website, but hardly it is described or depicted how much more its capability is. Indeed, these capabilities are categorized into distinct sections that are linked to anything from land use and property information to financial systems, from public goods and services to citizen relationship management and public safety (Augustsan 2001) (King 1982).

Significantly, information technology allows for provision of local e-Government services. It offers an excellent medium through which flow of information and transactions in enabled amongst local government and its stakeholders. Aspects for developing e-Government include:

1.   Information: Every aspect related to information and data must be taken into account, including legal infrastructure, data standards, data protection and privacy

2.   Technology Infrastructure: The network infrastructure and hardware have to be looked into; what are needed, what are currently available, and how to acquire them; and lastly

3.   Software and Tools: Software and Tools required to facilitate local e-Government must be identified, along with methods of acquiring them (Augustsan 2001).

There exist websites that allow people with disability to access Local and State Government websites. These websites not only provide online correspondence with local officials and

information about government services, but also allow renewal of library books and driver's licenses, provide tax information and accept tax returns, and apply for jobs and benefits. The importance of such websites lies in the fact that they offer disabled people:

1. programs and services in a more interactive and dynamic way to increase citizen participation
2. convenience in obtaining services or information
3. reduced costs in offering programs as well as information regarding government services
4. reduced amount of paperwork
5. Expansion of possibilities of offering new programs and reaching new communities (U.S. Department of Justice 2003).

Thus, Internet has being playing a critical role in facilitating government to serve in a better manner to all its citizens. Overall, governments are attempting to take full advantage of the recent technologies to achieve cost savings and to enable value-added transaction driven portals. Typically, they not only address routines/ processes that are repetitive, menial and involving communication, but also deal with decision indicative multi-department process flow paths, by which their shift to the web is capable of making a noticeable difference in the absence of big modifications to the existing work practices or to the IT infrastructure (Stenberg & Austin 2007) (U.S. Department of Justice 2003).

The conventional methods of work, organization and process flow techniques are witnessing a niche in this kind of portals. These portals mainly come under one of the three categories mentioned below:

1. Intranet applications which enable data to be gathered, shared and processes in new and efficient manner
2. Extranets the link Government and Business Partners bringing cost-savings and discipline to procurement
3. Public websites which offer a self-service channel to Citizens for their dealings with the government

Today, there exist several empirical studies regarding e-Government in practice as against the empirical research into commercial business in areas like internet marketing, enterprise computing, and electronic commerce, wherein there is wealth of academic and

business publications. But this scenario is gradually changing and there are a few noticeable exceptions to the paucity of e-Government research (Stenberg & Austin 2007).

The key findings extracted from the latest reports are the identification of various key international trends. The first trend is that business models belonging to local governments are gradually being enabled by newest technologies that is creating new possibilities of government services delivery and for the organization. Furthermore, this recursive innovation involving IT capabilities and business innovation is a well grounded concept of research into commercial organization; similar outcomes are being observed in government organizations as well (Holland & Cahill). The second trend indicates the increase in business and technology integration that are within a single government agency as well as amongst separate agencies. The third important trend identified was based on the rapidly growing sophistication of government services with respect to the scale and the breadth of the on-line government services, which resulted into urging leading governments to attempt to personalize services in the similar manner in which financial services companies and commercial retailers have implemented initiatives for offering services tailored to specific individual needs. Additionally, the most advanced e-Government institutions continue to grow in terms of stages of growth concept. These observations and results regarding the on-going improvement of services as well as sophistication related to the use IT propose that every e-Government program moves through distinctive phases of maturity and development (Holland & Cahill).

Identifying such unique phases of development, a project based on public affairs was established that sought to recognize those features that separated IT leaders from the laggards. This project was based upon a detailed survey of a wide spectrum of IT strategies among several states, cities, and countries. The leaders possessed many characteristics that differentiated them from the laggards; namely:

1. integrated IT architectures
2. explicit connection between managerial outcomes and IT strategies
3. evaluation of IT investments and sophisticated strategic planning
4. smart IT procurement
5. innovation concerning areas like e-democracy and innovation within service delivery
6. formal training activities

The IT architectures are based on how various information systems are integrated. Moreover, the advent of 3G technology has potential for expanding the levels of integration with mobile users (Holland & Cahill).

A good example of e-Government evolution is observed in Singapore that has been claimed as one of the world leaders in e-Government. The reasons behind the success of Singaporean e-Government is backed by the fact that Singapore is an e-Government innovator since a long period of time, which provides one of the best demonstrations of how a single government transits through the distinct phases of growth as it gets more sophisticated and knowledgeable about the use of e-Government processes and IT. One of the most essential outcomes of the early initiatives is the establishment of a standard IT infrastructure throughout all government agencies along with their wider eco-systems including business partners and suppliers. This, in turn, made it much easier to enforce the vision of "many agencies, one government" (Holland & Cahill).

Government ICT policy regarding e-Government can be an influential drive for local e-Government. Local e-Government's overall strategies and visions must be identified along with how e-Government is able to enable achievement of those strategies and visions. Moreover, the priorities of goals and objectives must be established and the rationales of local e-Government application and projects may require investigations (Holland & Cahill).

E-Gov Portals:

e-Gov portals indicate global points of entry to several different local services from distinctive public service providers. Consumers as well as public authorities are able to access these offers through the Internet or while on the move via electronic devices like handhelds, mobile phones, etc. Therefore, this forms the customer-focused or external view of public services. From the internal or government-specific perspective, the services are considered to be the sequence of process steps which should be performed by the entire system to satisfy customer requirements. Combining these two points of view is an essential matter in the modeling of public services offered via a global single-point of access orientation (Wimmer 2004). Many key aspects have to be dealt with for meeting this requirement:

- To find a suitable mapping terminology
- To apply a holistic concept for modeling public services

- To develop integrated service models which will cover both the front office and back offices
- To apply a service-centric and user-centric developing approach
- Adequately merging service models into the technical components of the platform.

Virtually, every e-Government technology is already working for e-commerce. For instance, Customer Relationship Management (CRM), Supply Chain Management (SCM), Enterprise Resource Management (ERP), Data Mining and Warehousing, Business Intelligence, Payment Systems and Internet Procurement. All need little adaptation for e-Government purposes. Similarly, multi-layered firewall, security protocols, as well as public key infrastructures required for protection and authentication of user data are available off the shelf. Also, the vendors who wish to offer patent solutions owned by them agree to the fact that technology is not a barrier to introduction of e-Government (Wimmer 2004) (King 1982).

Bibliography

Augustsan, A 2001, *Information Technology in Local Government: A Practical Guide for Managers*, International City/County Management Association, Washington, D.C.

Holland, C, & Cahill, M, *3G Technology in Local Government: Case Examples of Business Process Change and Strategic Innovation*, viewed 01 April, 2010, <http://www.mgovernment.org/resurces/euromgvo2006/PDF/15_Holland.pdf>.

Kim, H, & Bretschneider, S 2006, *Local Government Information Technology Capacity: An Exploratory Theory*, The Maxwell School, viewed 31 March, 2010, <http://cepa.maxwell.syr.edu/papers/47.html>.

King, J 1982, *Local Government Use of Information Technology: The Next Decade*, American Society for Public Administration, viewed 30 March, 2010, <http://www.jstor.org/pss/976089>.

Stenberg, C, Austin, S (eds.) 2007, *Managing Local Government Services*, International City/ County Management Association (ICMA), Washington, D.C.
Wimmer, M (ed.) 2004, *Knowledge Management in Electronic Government*, Springer, New York.
U.S. Department of Justice 2003, *Accessibility of State and Local Government Websites to People with Disabilities*, U.S. Department of Justice, viewed 31 March, 2010, <http://www.ada.gov/websites2_prnt.pdf>.